# Floodwater

Dear Luke,

With much

Admiration &

Appreciation

Best always

[signature]

Cover & Interior art, watercolor: Melinda B Hipple
Cover design: Steven Asmussen & Tracy McQueen
Design & Layout: Katherine Herschler

Glass Lyre Press, LLC.
P.O. Box 2693
Glenview, IL 60026
www.GlassLyrePress.com

# Floodwater

Connie Post

# Foreword

Passages in "Floodwater," the title poem of Connie Post's exciting new collection, wash up in me vivid images of Welsh writer Elaine Morgan's Aquatic Ape, as she called our ancient, ocean-spawned ancestor. With seasoned courage and in ever-renewable language, the poet guides us through the inner houses, backyards, closets, rivers, creeks, dreamscapes, landscapes she inhabits and into the things she loves, lyricizing it against the boil and bubble of everyday newsroom terror. And throughout these reflections, ruminations and inspirations, Post never stops picturing earth and sky and day and night as sentient beings, extensions of our own bodies and psyches. "To Iraq" whispers with sympathy to a country raped; "Sierra Leone" addresses the rape of a particular girl and systemic rape worldwide; "Their Plane Crashed Into a Cemetery in Montana" asks: "If the earth had language / would it translate / the dialect of endings?"; and "Jaycee Lee Dugard Bore Children of Kidnapper" opens onto a couplet that haunts: "… interviews crowd the airwaves / like clotted blood // She is alive!" How far into the light have we former fish journeyed since our forebears first swam up on shore from the sea? Floodwater asks this, and so much else, while its intimate pages trouble and lull us, pulling us under its spell.

**Al Young**
California's poet laureate emeritus

# Contents

# Floodwater

All the rooms in the house
are flooding
but there is no water

all of the people are drowning
but the lifeguard
is in an irreversible coma

we walk around
as if floating matters
as if there is a surface
to find

we look for a syringe of air,
a breathing tube of decency
but there are barely audible gasps
that pretend to be language

there are lost fish
swimming at our feet

it's as if only the walls understand
why we get the bends every morning
when we rise too fast

it's as if
the last boat
has pulled up its anchor

we sink to the bottom,
grow gills
and swim past the lifeguard
who has forgotten
how to survive
in a room
with no air

# Structurally Sound

I hear strange sounds in the night
but you tell me
"it's just the sounds that old houses make"

but the ceiling and I know better

this house was built too fast
the concrete was poured too soon
the foundation set wrong
the floorboards are held together
with daily acts of contrition

we know how quickly
walls were erected
how the hands of strong men
forced the frame upward
even while their muscles frayed

we know what it means to hide
know the support beams will fall someday
we know the roof will eventually be condemned
along with the rest of the dwelling

for now
I walk carefully upon
the hardwood floors
listening for frailties
for creaking unnoticed by others

I hide under rickety door frames
find cracks in places nobody knows about
trying to tell you
again
again
how hard it can be
to hide inside a body

# Breathing Room

Go to the darkest room in your house
find the nights you dropped
like futile music
stay there
until something shaped like a hand
taps you on the shoulder
and tells you to move to the corner
knowing the ceiling is cracking

brush the falling dust from your hair
as if it were hunger
or another faint emptiness that comes from
the center

find the walls
that you painted all through last winter
and stand with your back to each still sticky
until the color
peels like forgiveness you cannot give

look for the deliberate indentations,
in spite of the stolen light
and remember the rooms
you were commanded to
even when doors were swollen, closed,
slammed
nailed shut in spite of
all the remorse of a candle-lit house

after you spend years there,
you will find notes
stuck inside the grooves of the floor
they will look like scraps of music
pretend to be words

but in the dark
only you will understand
how sound was born
you will feel the floor open
beneath you
find a Stradivarius waiting there

you will play until your neck hurts
until every string breaks
as if you already knew
how a room becomes a silence

## 5.6 Earthquake

The reports said
there had not been one of this magnitude
in over ten years
I realized – that's how long
we have not spoken,
probably longer

As the crystal in the china cabinet
shook like glaciers before they fall,
I thought I heard the phone ring
–it was you calling to see if everything
was okay
but the ground was not finished
shifting
it went on until the plates cracked
the clock fell
and the phone never rang

I don't know if the glasses can still
carry cool water
or if they will leak when summer comes
at night, I wonder if I will be able to
hold each stem without breaking

I don't know how long it went on
really it was more like a long sleep
where waking is false
and the ground never loved you anyway

# Loss of Appetite

I was hungry once

I let the earth's crust
melt over my tongue

I ate the equator
like bread with no edges
and the world was mine

I let the polar ice caps
slip past my throat
like the coldest snow cone
crystalline and blue

I was thirsty once
before there was salt
in the ocean

I was the sky
I was unbroken
I was a century unseen

today
I carry worry beads
–pray at the altar
of starvation

I think about broken countries
follow the fault lines
–watch the plates shift
mercilessly

rinse my mouth
with salt water

I was hungry once

# If

What if all the trees were stone
And all stones
wood

would all the river bottoms
turn brown with aging bark
leaves clogging the paths to oceans

firs and redwood falling
cracking the ground
like columns from Rome
societies ending with merely the sound
of their own collapse

if everything fell the wrong way
backwards and into the sky
how would the clouds
hold their shape
would we know
how to patch the sky

how would we know
where the moon belonged

if my skin turned inside out
and all my bones were
made of dry clay and dirt
would the earth finally
see each uprooted tree
and understand
how a forest dies

# After Dinner

On the back porch with the dog
breathing steadily next to me
I listen for the sounds in the night
only he can hear

the crows have come back again
and his ears move like a symphony
as the blackest of birds fly over us

I remember that only fourteen days ago
I had no dog
no other way of knowing
how to breathe

but he wandered into a wide street
—then into my back yard
then into the back rooms
of my psyche

now – on summer evening walks
he synchronizes
his steps with mine
makes a telepathy
of old pathways

as if he understands
how stern the dark asphalt can be
as if he knows
why I often stumble on the driveway

and when he looks at me
before I remove his leash
I wonder how
he has so easily
found his way beneath the fences
the gates I thought I had closed

how forgiveness finds a small
edge
a thin slat
to glide through

# A Road of My Own

I want a road of my own
where the stones
have not been counted

I want to walk on dirt
that has fallen from
the back side of reality

where the soil is the color
of shaman's blood

I need to hold a compass
that has forgotten the way home
and points south of shame

I want to travel with a satchel
that only I can clutch

inside, there will be hats and
a thousand scarves
made for covering
the turquoise stones of history

inside, there will be
crumpled maps
never folded back
the way they were given to me

I will take them out only at dusk
find the midpoint
between gratitude and rage
head the other direction

I will walk over silenced gravel
until I remember how
to find the Braille beneath ground

I will sigh as my satchel drops away
I will undo the shoulder strap of scorn
and finally,
breathe the dust of my own footsteps

# Growing Distance

When someone drives away from you
forever
what is that distance that grows
as they disappear

for years, you can feel it inside you
the space expands, forces you to walk off center
but you tell your friends
you are just tired

leave parties too early
with your coat hanging
half around your waist

later – when everyone has gone to bed
you sort through granules of your sleep
to find the time before they left
before the ground slipped
from your hands

you find yourself
running in a garden
pruned too thin

the night grows old
breathes only when you do
and as always,
Smells like damp air before thunder

you may find torn maps
all over your yard
you may hide them from yourself – again and again
but they always lead you
to the same moment
parked in front of your own misery

again, at the same narrow garden
staring at the worn trellis
humming a requiem
wondering why your tombstone
is there
without your name

# What Does Loss Smell Like

It smells like nothing at all

not the damp air

or the wet leaves outside

it severs itself

from your half-burnt incense


it remembers nothing about sacraments

and can't pretend to be fog

I wish I could tell someone

how you faded away one day
back when I was rain

but since the dirt on my shoes has dried
I can't smell a thing

not even the crisp shirt you left

drying on the chair out back

# Advice to the Dog Sitter

Remember the house key
is never where you left it

remember the pull of the leash
and how it  reminds you
of the long sinew of muscle

remember how to zip your coat
with one hand

remember he is a stray
that he has only been with us
for thirty-six days

remember sometimes
he does not believe
the truth in the cracks of night
or that we will wake
in the morning
and offer sustenance

remember how your whole self
can be found in the fur
at the underside of his neck

remember that language
is the illusion of intimacy
how a tepid silence
has a buoyancy of its own

remember there is mercy
in your broken hands
and he will pull from you
whatever you have to offer

# Service Call at 4 p.m.

You enter my house
with a tool box
as if that will fix everything

as if that annoying noise
will be stifled
and there will be
no screws losing their threads

as if you could fix an oven
that has burned
for years

as if you could
tinker with a washer
that has cleansed
too many thin undergarments

the water  heater is screaming
and the pilot light
has crashed

there is no warm water
left in this century

the faucets have all rusted
with the orange of a crumbling autumn

and you are standing here
in the hallway
searching for a crow bar
a drill
a sturdy platform of granite

anything that might
help me lift these
broken beams
that look too much
like my splintered bones

## Just Before the Day Ends

Never walk alone at dusk

the crows will land
too close
scrutinize the way you walk
under the low hanging branches

they will watch your every breath
and you will both
understand
why the day singes
at its edge

you will count your steps
until you finally arrive
at your front door

find the porch light off
your whole house
leaning towards the night

a citadel
of dwindling mercy

# Mouthful

I drank the sky today

emulsified blue
frosty, hazy shake
melting in my paper cup

clouds so thick
they stuck in my straw

so cold, I froze my forehead

I polished it off
in ten minutes
ingesting the wing of a lost bird,
a tornado never descended

it was the last item
on the menu
in a café of crumbling counters

it was the last chance
for a horizon to feign liquidity

as the quiet, small framed
cashier
handed me the cup

I asked her to drink with me
but she turned away

told me
from the silence of her swollen back

that not moments ago
she swallowed
the last crumb of earth

## Just After Seven

I step into our room
to grab a sweater
the light is already fading
you have pulled the blinds

I pause and notice

the fiber of dark
how it remembers
all the hours we've  spent here
lying in half-curled positions

it holds the filaments of whisper
absorbs the way you tell me
"remember, I'm here"
right before you drift off

we both know
you can't enter the dreams
of my own dying
or feel the way night wraps
itself in tight bands
around the tourniquet of dawn

but the blackness knows
stares at me
tells me
all I have is your
steady breath

it is enough
even when I am certain,
every lamp on earth
is broken

it is enough
until I find warmer nights
feel the fabric
atone for this
crumbling citadel
of bleeding light

## Self Exam

It starts in the shower
warm, unexpected
like June rain

one dedicated drop runs down the open meadow
finds the crevasse of flesh and indecision
and reminds you again, it's time

it finds its way, slowly
forcing the soap into a known lather

you close your eyes
separate flesh and fear
as they splinter to a node
a slight swelling you don't remember
from last time.....

feeling for slight changes in topography
folding each thought between the fingers

each moment becomes a mother, aunt, sister
a mastectomy, a passing worry
an unhealed incision
an unborn regret

all of the  malignancies cascading down the body
into the stainless steel drain of latent stories

the water running down
through the holes
through the unknown holes
where you never look

the soap thin and fragile,
breaks apart in your hands
like the shape it cannot hold
as you press back for swollen knowledge

praying for mercy in the steam
–a way to towel dry anxiety
long after
the water has run dry

# Long Night

The roof
made with old stucco
breathes

you stare at it
all night
wonder when the
child will be born
push through
the uterus

time and time again
you have forced
these un-named babies
into the world

travelers between
an amniotic history
and a broken equator

you check to see
if the room is dilated
if you can again
birth your duende
with no midwife

and again
you find yourself breech
no way
to push the womb
back into the century
to which you were born

## Low Tide

You dropped this moon
so suddenly
so many years ago
and left it this way

I pass by
on occasional autumns
when there is nothing
left of me

I try to understand
why you never saw
the large cracks in the sky
the way the salt-blue sea
bears down on itself

you say it is the ocean's fault
tell me often
how it stole gravity from you
but I am standing here
with sand pouring out of my mouth

putting myself under these rocks
trying to make you understand
this is the first moon
I ever loved

# Summer Gone

She swears she will never
remove this dress

at least not from over the shoulder
and never before midnight

only when fall has turned away
only when the window
does not notice her
leaving like solstice

will she find the fabric
from which it was made

she will kneel
at the wooden chest
at the foot of her bed

call up the gods of fabric
and languid August skies

she loves pulling out the patterns again
feeling the thin paper, as if it were a sky
yet to be made

she will again remember the store clerk
cutting the cloth so carefully
as if it were a shadow

the effortless folding
its scent, nestled inside
the creased paper bag

she will kneel
for the longest time
again, understand
the simple kindness of a shoulder strap
the way faded cotton
can remember a falling moon

she will carefully hide
the hem lines of summer

quietly tucking in
each edge
like a prayer

# Constellation

There are stars in our veins
ones that have flickered out
seen the end of all moons
fallen under the back side of the galaxy

there are meteors in the pulse of the neck
waiting to fall from the body
waiting for a chance to burn a hole in the villages of hands,
pelvic bones, feet, locked knees

they fall from us like chaos
like words that burn the roofs of mouths
leave the skin of regret hanging

we drink the cold water, swish it around our cheeks
as if ice particles know how to dissolve shame
as if steam will rise from our mouths
there are days when celestial bodies tumble – bones crack
everything falls below the etched sky line
implodes
the serum of generations falls
leaks through a fibrous universe

the blood can no longer return to the center
the circling of all fluid ceases
all the suns of thoughts, planets, arteries
burn
dissipate
the particles of selves
reabsorbed into a vague chance
of a remembered life

we step off, look back from a reverent ledge
the orbit slowing, hesitant
we turn away,
step down the brittle constellation

take a last glimpse
and remember an Indian summer night sky
stars sprinkling down
and a voice from over your shoulder
a voice from the village
whispers

"There is a place where the light bends"

## Winter has stepped
## through the front door again

Everything is melting
but the snow

language
confluence
the idea of solid ground

like a church choir off key,
I try to speak
but find only fractured words
fallen from the mouth I was given

I am looking for the snowy owl
the blending of white to white
the delicate turning of a god-like neck

I walk through the still
forest of our last conversation
and can't find solace in one syllable

I promised I would come to find you
even if you left forever

I am putting on my thin coat
my shredded gloves

I open a scarf
like the ways I cannot unfold you

I step onto the black ice
pray that it knows the Braille
of my admonished feet

I walk inside a night that has
never forgiven me for being born

I step over the carcass of a screech owl
its bones
silenced by snow

# Perimeters

November is swollen

the winter months
are leaking backward
into the borders of fall

the days bulge with remorse
fall off the calendar
until the floor is streaming
with currents

I stand in front of
what used to be Tuesday
but now the whole page is blank
–all I see are weeks
merging into one another
lines blurring

water rushes in
surrounds my bare feet
covers my knees, then waist
finally I am up to my chin
in fluid regret

people yell at me from other rooms
tell me how to backstroke out
but I don't know how to swim
any better than I did when I was eleven
don't know how to push all this water
out of my lungs
and find September again
with you standing there
still alive
a stone's throw away
from this broken equinox

and your voice always telling me
"you can drown in four feet of water"

# Fire Line

The fire starts like a bad conversation
spreading through wilderness
jumping from one tree to another

people watch from miles away
the smoke rising
like sin from a body

weeks later
the charred earth remains
like a welt on the land

eventually the soil understands
the language of submission
how to stay quiet when night comes

planes will fly overhead
noticing the edges of black
–how a loss is contained

as summer leaves
the fields seem to heal
the deepest green seeps to the surface
like old discolored blood from a bruise

everyone is quiet for a while
months pass
everyone forgets
drives by the quiet hills
as if they are redeemed

then in fall
the rain begins
continues on and on
like a story without chapters

how easily a mud slide happens
how easily a mind succumbs

and when they come to look for you
they will have to move
the granules of earth aside
with their bare and swollen hands

# Fire Escape

I think I could find this door
if flames were everywhere

I think I could find
the small exit sign
if orange held the
scorching words
crackling out of a mouth

your mouth
to be exact

I swear my elbows
could carry me across
this flat room
even if I had to hold my breath

but no one told me
I would need a crowbar
for the door

I keep reminding myself
I left you in my twenties
but find myself sitting, sometimes
in the same armchair
looking out a half-open window
screaming fire
when no one else
is in the room

## "Their Plane Crashed into a Cemetery in Montana"

**cnn.com**
**March 23, 2009**

If the earth had arms
would they have encircled the plane
held it close

smothered the flames
with its own blanket

if the earth had language
would it translate
the dialect of endings

would the scattered flowers
around the gravesites
remember how they too
were brought here
carried by shaking hands
then – left behind on a
crumbling Saturday afternoon

how each stem
was plucked from the ground
too soon

how each yearned
for the placenta of soil

each one knowing
how to break
into bloom
like a body
upon arrival

# "Let It Be"

When I was nine
Paul McCartney's voice
seeped through the bottom cracks
of all the doors in the house

"When I find myself in times of trouble"
how a young girl plays
the same music in her room
as if the singer knows
her name
her crumpled, simple thoughts

"Mother Mary comes to me"
how a young girl
believes the man inside
the record player knows
when she is taking off her dress

"Whisper words of Wisdom"
how a man's voice can understand
there is no mother
no words
no rosary bead
sturdy enough for this heavy a prayer

"Let it Be, Let it Be"
and she does
let it be, only to let it fall
as she swallows the rosary
the beads, the cross
the song

and it crumbles
like the lyrics
that broke in her hand
upon learning
how to leave a  room

# "Jaycee Lee Dugard Bore Children of Kidnapper Lived in Backyard"

**Mercury News August 28, 2009**

All day the lead reporter ends each segment with
"she is alive"

interviews crowd the airwaves
like clotted blood

She is alive

She will vomit the tar of night each morning
She will kneel at dawn
like a sacrament she can't swallow

She is alive

She will stack her limbs
like dry wood
before she leaves a room
the termites already
feasting on her bones

She is alive

the story will fade
the dry rot of years will pass

the schizophrenic birds
will fly blind in the slanted sky

she will bend her neck and watch them
but no one else will notice

nor will they notice the tar leaking
from her mouth

they will nod as they pass
and simply say to themselves

She is alive

# Left Behind

you dropped your promise
on the way out the door

I noticed it hanging
half out of your pocket
when you came in

I could tell you had a life
full of hard whiskey
and imperfect chapters

you never looked at me
as I sat reading a magazine
about health and wellness

your appointment was before mine
so I never heard your name

I wonder what you told
your children before
you left them in the dry heat
of Arizona

I wonder how many
burned bars and broken teeth
you have stepped over
between the red chili pepper skies

it's not that
you remind me of anyone

it's not that I shuddered
when your hand smothered
the door knob when you left

it's only that
I have picked up this
promise you left behind
and it is still here in my lap

but who am I to pretend
I've ever seen a red pepper sky
or that my teeth have ever
been broken

# Contortionist

She takes one foot
then the other
and folds each behind her head

even her marrow bends,
but it doesn't seem to matter
to anybody
what creases are left in the body
after the show is over

all that matters
is the audible gasp
the disbelief
the way a crowd
pretends to understand edges

when she unfolds her spine
long after everyone has gone
she will tell herself
that young boy
she left back in that southern town
really did love her
that he wanted to make her happy
to take her away
from these sticky cotton candy nights

but he could not understand
the narrow curve of her back
her quiet fraying muscles and
the silence mixed in between

another August has come and gone
she lies still now in her thin bed
waiting to succumb to sleep
waiting to forget about flexion
and the forgeries of the body

–how so many nights ago
long before autumn was orange
her whole body
became a sacrilege

# The Man in Front of the Pharmacy

Plays the guitar
a Spanish ballad I barely recognize
I slip over his voice on the pavement
tripping on lyrics and averted gazes

I lay a few dollar bills
in his guitar case
but know I should have also put
my bones inside

maybe he could sing them unbroken
maybe he sees in me
the marrow of songs I have
swallowed since birth

maybe he understands
the way a guitar pick
can remind someone
of exile
the way the strings
stay separated

before I leave
he nods quietly
–thanks me with his dark eyes

I look at him one last time
and realize
we both understand
this long hairline fracture
on the back side of autumn

## Loose Change

All of the telephone booths
are disappearing

the sidewalks
have forgotten how to
speak

there will be no businessmen
finding shelter
during the rain
calling wives, girlfriends
kids they have forgotten

people will pass and never
notice him crying into the receiver
saying he never meant
for it to turn out this way

there will be no mothers
making sure their daughters
have dimes, quarters
– a pocket with no holes

the hinges have rusted
like years we cannot close
the curbs are growing
and there is no place for
old women to put on their coats
after dusk

there is nowhere to go
when you need
one person to hand you
a slim coin, nod silently
and understand

watch you close
the thin doors around you

## Folding

We once folded
the same beige blanket
each night
before bed

you taking one end
me the other

you taught me how to tuck in
the corners
assure it was oblong
and perfect
like your straightened apron

finally
after two steps
to the center
we would meet

I watched carefully
how you would complete the act
—such relief and retribution
in finding order

in the stepping away
I always wondered if you knew
how empty my hands felt after
they dropped to my side

in leaving the room
I understood how quiet
was folded and put away

today
I find myself turning in the edges
of frayed hours

I spend each night
waiting for an ordinary dusk
to meet me
somewhere in the middle

# I Need to Make Something

A voice repeats
in my head all morning
as I wander the aisles
of the craft store

it's been three weeks since the funeral
I decide I should get out for at least a while

I pick up
masks that break when I touch them
construction paper that turns to dust
paint brushes that have no bristles

it can't be with yarn
or string
or things that untie

it has to be the same color as
the lipstick I used to steal
from your dresser
but there are no pastels
or oils in that shade

I find only rows of plastic flowers
pretending to have authentic stems
pretending they can root themselves
in the flower pot
beneath my kitchen window

I find a thousand colors
of origami paper I cannot fold
into the same story

it all comes back as loss

the cashier looks at me
like I'm crazy
as she counts back my change
and tries to understand
why I've purchased every false flower
in the store
as if they too – could pretend
we are perennial

# Driving Down this Old Road

I still see you
sitting on the back porch
putting on your work boots
glaring at me
as if I had sinned for being young

I wondered why
you sat there, for so long
before you left for work

fastening each leather lace
as if it were a sacrament

each morning
you would leave me
and my dented Charlie Brown
lunch pail
waiting for the bus,
the milk in the thermos
already turning warm
the bread hardening

I can still hear the gravel
beneath the bus tires
as if each stone
knew the weight of a child


as I walk paved streets
more often these days

my feet hurt every night

I look back and realize,
you already understood
the ground,
how the earthworms
were laced inside of it

how they were begging
for quieter steps
from you and I

# Shell Store

I find the bin with the sea urchin spines
thin
delicate
a resonance of moons and tides.
they fall through my fingers,
as you have

I listen intently to the sounds
of each one
rubbing against another
my hand mixing them
like gravel and sorrow

they sound like old beads from a
secret rain dance

the chant follows me
a ritual barely memorable
but carried under the skin

I see the medicine doctors' prayers
in between each shell-shaped shadow
between the fingers
I pretend to own

I cannot stop my hands from moving
or follow the exact way
they seem to understand
extraction, death

even as you call to me
from the store's entry way
I do not answer

you are leaving
moving on to the salt water taffy shop

but I stand here
frozen
wondering who am I
to believe I can blend
the spines of creatures
who only saw the world
from shallow water

# How to Eat a Crab

Understand first
that the shells
are as delicate as sorrow

learn how
to break the weakest points
– find ways to avoid
unwanted splinters
– drop them secretly
beneath the table

or they will find their way past your lips
and poke the caverns
of your foreign mouth

hammer out the sounds
of your succulent remorse
and pull from the meat
of your shredded thoughts

as everyone leaves the dormant dinner table
chant a forgotten nocturne
while the empty shells
forget the sound of their own cracking

fold the tablecloth
with all of the remains
of the fractured ocean

kneel at the shoreline
until only sand
is falling from your mouth

## Skeletal Structure

I have mispronounced the names
of all the bones in my body

clavicle
comes out "clamor"

femur
comes out "famine"

pelvis
comes out   "paleontology"

I have tried to untie
the slip knot in my own tongue
but pulling at it
makes it worse

my teeth
lined up
like a stalwart fence
will not let the syllables form

syntax pools at the ledge
of my swollen gums

everyone tells me to enunciate
– that the words will take shape

but they don't understand
how my bones have never forgiven me
for those elongated years of silence

so I spend my nights
stammering on the phone
trying to find a translator
someone who understands
the etiology of a ruined mind

someone who can repeat for me
the epilogue of the body

marrow
    amnesia
        fracture

# Extremities

You can lose body parts
crossing a city street

you can lose your hands
inside the outstretched arms
of a woman's cardboard sign
disappear inside another country

you can lose your feet
inside the tap dancer's shoes,
the click, click, click on the pavement
a way to measure the world
as it falls away
in incremental eight counts

you can lose your skin to the wind
it finds the exact place where
your pores are most open

you can lose your organs
as they carefully fall outside of you
while you step into a cross walk

you can lose your brain as the pigeons
fly over you
as the taxi cab runs too close to the curb
and never understand why you were built
like this
barely sustainable
commanded to stay whole
while stepping over
your swollen self

as if all those pieces you've
picked up along the way
were never you

# Search Party

Send out the cadaver dogs
barking
salivating

send them every day
until you think you know me

but you will not find me here
in this field of dry grass

I started dismembering myself
years ago

my arms belong to countries
where other wars still burn

my legs belong to the ocean
where salt is marrow
full of cord and knotted blood cells

my teeth are stuck in Stonehenge
chipped and shaved down
in the prongs of slanted history

autumn will come and go
you will find only small bone fragments,
on this fallow clearing of land

you will find small trinkets that
look like a broken mind
but you will discard them as you did me

at night
the dogs will eat quietly on your back porch
sleep and dream about
this death I could not give you

# In Stitches

I have cut out the same pattern
on the same table
in the same small room
where no one can hear me

I have stitched the seams
with all the symmetry of a measured life
and assured the curtains are closed

I have counted each thread
and made sure the spool holds
the long silk of memory
I have made sure each color
is a word I dare not say

but even as I pull together
all the finishing touches
I still don't recognize these portraits
of cloth and dark lace

I step back and realize
I have dropped too many pins
made too many loose patches

but I know I must leave this place
soon
and everyone expects to see
something emerge

so I will loosen the two scarves
from each neck
make sure I can hold my sewn selves
with two hands

knowing I am the only one
who will understand
why I made

one to keep

one to give away

## Voices of Schizophrenia

There are birds
I will bring
that will fly crooked
in the bent sky

their feathers are matted
with the screaming spit
of the gods

they have flown here
from a foreign land
to tell you

all those times
they landed
on the sacred lake
of sanity

were never
for you

# Sister of a Schizophrenic

She knows his words
are spoken in the dialect
of crumbling

for the fourth time this week
she descends the stairs
brings a half warm meal
and sets it on the night stand

he hasn't eaten in three days

the ham in the club sandwich
is starting to curl at the edges
she tucks it in
hoping he will only see
the pristine, white bread
kneaded by the hands of a baker
who has never known madness

she prays he will like
the dark chocolate cupcakes
–that he will take all three pills
in the folded paper cup

and look at her again
as if they shared
the same hunger

# Asymmetry

What if you
were only
your own reflection

standing there
looking at your life
from within the mirror

watching yourself
pass back and forth

hanging up clothes
folding towels
putting yourself
in the drawer
when no one is looking

would you forget
the coarse, heavy blankets,
the dreams
that burn your skin

would your tongue
fold back into itself
until you finally understood
mimes, their gloved hands,
their painted faces


would you reach out
your own hand
motion yourself
to look under the bed

and find your own silence
waiting there
gathering dust

# Lost in Flight

Last night, a moth followed me in
from the dark
I didn't notice it,
until I turned on the light

its wings panicked
inside the harshly lit room

its flight, unmapped,
unrhymed,
filling me with the dread
of the uncovered body of night

I tried to show a path not known,
but still, it didn't follow

the urgency of its flapping body
made me look away
as if it understood
how light holds no mercy

each wing beating against an uneven surface
a dialect of a lost civilization
leading me back to dark sanctuaries
the rooms we enter and exit

I kept thinking I heard the frantic creature
pushing up against my bedroom wall.
I kept believing it had a mouth

I opened the back door, one last time
and finally it slipped away

I turned down the blinds
walked back to my bed
watched my hands crumble
like the  forgiveness
I cannot give
for having ever opened the window
to see you standing there
broken,
wingless at last

# Recognition

Ten thousand years ago
would you have recognized me

would you have heard the wind of servitude
in a low hummed song beneath the earth
would you have lifted your head from an old night
and noticed me
gathering food from a field far away

would you see the loose clothing
hanging off center, between stones and survival
would you notice me kneeling
even when no one asked
as I crouched to pick up acorns and beetles

would you see the sagging breasts
the anguish that looked like sky
the babies I birthed and lost

would you have recognized
the cadence of my tousled hair
moist tendrils in the mouth
pulled inside the body
like a field of sin

would you walk towards me
through yellow and faded grass
push aside the mute stalks
that seemed to know
one day
you would come for me
lead me towards the cave
of your open mouth

the tongue of memory
pushing me out
into this moment
still looking for your tombstone
before there was a chisel
a way to shape the stones

# Sierra Leone

*"Dona Nobis Pacem"*
*—Latin: Grant us Thy Peace*

Your name drops out of a mouth
like a cappella
but the violinists wait
in case another sound is needed

the vocalist strains on a stage far away
trying to raise itself one octave above its own sins

the story of a rape of a ten-year-old girl
is told again
each time a shredded map
falls

the pathways of its own life
burns unto itself
for itself
for the sake of backwards silence

I walk down the streets of my town
wondering where I might hide
if I were a young girl in Sierra Leone

I hear my own footsteps like a loss
that has its own rhythm

how can a place
that sounds like music
become its own obituary
flapping in the wind,
behind a stone that will not turn over

the counted carats of a lost country
cut through the glass of our distilled and measured shame

all this looking away
wondering where the last singer has gone

someday finding her too, alone
as she rocks incessantly
sings
over and over
"dona nobis pacem"
in the dark

# To Iraq

*"Kyrie eleison"*
*–Greek for "Lord Have Mercy"*

I think of you most often at night
when the ground is silent

I think of you when darkness invades
when I can't roll over
without waking my own subconscious

there is an empty vase on the dresser
that makes a strange reflection in the dark
I wonder if it is Baghdad, telling me
it is trying to live

I wonder if it is another ending
I cannot see

I feel your wounds open on my skin
and press to close them
but the gauze falls away
like peace

there is a small light across the street
that calls to me
begging to know why I can fall sleep
but you cannot

why the ceilings of a mosque
have crumbled again

It is eleven p.m.
and all I see in the dark
is the hand of a small boy
reaching
reaching out
pulling himself from the rubble

but I cannot grab the hand
for it is the shape of a country
and each finger is broken
I find small sticks, frantically glue them together
but am told in ancient languages,
there is no splint for remorse

I cannot find a way to
mend the quilts
of each torn twilight

I keep going back
each night
waking in the rubble
of crushed stone

I want to say I'm sorry
but your sons and daughters are gone
and even the mosque has not stopped weeping

as the night coagulates
I keep remembering a prayer
I was taught in Sunday school

I keep saying it,
to myself
even though I know the sky
cannot hear it

Kyrie eleison
Lord Have Mercy on Us
Kyrie eleison
when I butter my toast in the morning
Kyrie eleison
when I see the same boy's hand
who cannot find even bread or atonement

Kyrie eleison
for the sun
who will someday swallow this earth
and the ground
who will no longer
be silenced

# Old Woman in My Room

An old woman on the cover of a poetry book
watches over me at night

she is of Palestine

I set her on a night stand
near the lamp
where the light is uneven, slanted
she hovers like the scent of jasmine
outside the low window

her cratered skin spills stories across the air
her depleted expression
seeps into the hardwood floors
tells me the way she was scorned
and dropped away
like a piece of cloth
from burnt skin
the way her war-torn country
kneels inside her eyes
waiting for borders
to crumble like an early memory

waiting for jagged fences
to remember the gray regions of her hair
where she has planted olive trees
in the soil of uncultivated penance

she is of the River Jordon
its water finding no end
she is the decades of shorn sheep
the wool fallen
gathered
sold

she is the scattered flour
on the clay floors of ignorance
– her weeping runs only
to the bottom edge of the book
ceases, abruptly

I go to bed at night
my eyes already closed
she watches me, as I count the hooves of naked sheep
tossing, turning
under fine wool blankets
that have forgotten, like me, how to sleep

# Not Like the Rest

I have never had a pedicure
I do not want anyone else
hovering around my feet
– to come close enough
to smell the blood I have walked upon
from the roads of centuries passed
I am too afraid, they will find
ancient bone fragments between my toes,
realize I am not from this time

I imagine their solemn faces
pretending I am like the rest
asking me about my children's ages
or, if I will get my hair done tomorrow
I will look away
as they slowly understand
that my hair is coated with the marrow
of other wars
my skin has been nailed shut with
the thorns of a burnt rose bush

I keep my feet covered
pull them away from the clamor
of absolved hands
I go to bed at night and feel soldiers
rise and fall beneath my bed
they eventually lie silent, as do I
but each morning
I wake to hot coals
placed in distinct lines across
the floor of my bedroom

I avoid them
on the way to the shower
but traveling back
I fall – and later must explain
to the mute man at the grocery counter
why my hands
are burned beyond recognition

# Incantation

There is a an old church
at the end of a dirt road
inside each of us

even if we never prayed
never believed in god
we found places
to kneel
when no one else is looking
found a way to open the heavy door,
look inside and at least wonder
who built the altar

we have folded our hands quietly
while the field beside us has burned
we have said grace
while our bones break

after we walk over the sacrament
of a gravel path
we may even pause
look up at the trees
and remember why
they took a vow of silence

once every winter
we may leave the house
before anyone is awake
step carefully across
the burnt offerings of dawn

meander across a field
with too much undergrowth
and finally remember why
we've forgotten
how to genuflect
in the stillness

# In the Dressing Room

Trying on colors
neither the sky
nor I
were meant to own

I wonder if a partition
can make a difference
when light demands so much

there are shades
I've held too close
that should never
touch my skin

when turquoise is a lie
you come to know the precise way
clothing drops
from your knees
your waist
pulled like a shadow
over a pulsing throat

loose thoughts
fall from my back pocket
there are half-sewn seams
in the middle of my body

there are voices from
over the wall
I should listen to
but I don't

instead, I stand here
and wonder why I keep trying on
these countless garments –
destined for other bodies
more naked than mine

# Long Haul

When your sleep
is the heaviest thing
you've carried all day
you must remember
how to position it
how to tuck it under your chin

when everything is lost
in the gravity of dark
you must act normal
when the doorman offers
to help carry your bags

when large sacks of insomnia
are balanced
like groceries on your hip
you must learn
where the benches are,
how to settle in
between old ladies
and homeless men
rest with the pigeons
until dusk

you must step over
the sand man who is now
a war veteran, holding a tin cup

you must find places
to set the dark down
before the bag breaks,

before your nocturne
is scattered across a wide street

and you are left
on your muddied knees,
with no way to sort through
the dark figs, split oranges
rolling down a side alley
where you once prayed

## Standing in Front of a
## Painting at a Local Art Show

Each color holds a story
a language in which
a shade
has not yet been translated

a pathway where red splays
its journey
across a makeshift sky

each brush stroke
forms a dialect
not yet discovered

every blend calls to
a civilization
buried by the centuries

a banished woman
may walk out of the sea
her own hieroglyphics
and find herself naked
lost
standing silent before the
splatter of each of her lives
and not one
she will recognize
as herself

Grateful acknowledgment to the editors of the following journals which published or accepted these poems for publication:

*Adanna – Premier Issue:* "In The Dressing Room"

*Apparatus Magazine:* "Long Night"

*Arsenic Lobster:* "Search Party"

*Barnwood International:* "Asymmetry"

*Bloodroot Literary Review:* "Let It Be", "Loss of Appetite", "Jaycee Lee Dugard Bore Children of Kidnapper", "Skeletal Structure", "Perimeters" (Third Prize in Annual Award Winter 2012)

*Blue Fifth Review:* "In Stitches"

*Caesura 2010 – "5.6 Earthquake" (Winner of the Caesura 2009 Award)*

*California Quarterly:* "Their Plane Crashed into a Cemetery in Montana"

*California Quarterly:* "Sister of a Schizophrenic"

*Calyx – "Left Behind" (Runner-up, 2008 Lois Cranston Awards)*

*Clackamas Literary Review:* "Fire line", "Voices of Schizophrenia", "Not Like the Rest"

*Cold Mountain Review:* "Driving Down this Old Road"

*Comstock Review:* "Flood Water", "Structurally Sound", "Advice to the Dog Sitter"

*Convergence:* "Summer Gone", "Folding"

*DMQ Review:* "Just After Seven"

*I 70 Review:* "After Dinner"

*Karamu:* "Mouthful"

*Main Street Rag:* "A Road of My Own"

*Marin Poetry Center Anthology:* "Service Call at 4 p.m.", "Shell Store"

*Oberon:* "Loose Change", "Breathing Room", "Winter has stepped through the front door again"

*Palooka:* "Fire Escape", "Recognition"

*Pedestal Magazine:* "If"

*Pirene's Fountain:* "Extremities"

*Psychic Meatloaf:* "Just Before the Day Ends"

*SlipStream:* "How to Eat a Crab"

*Snail Mail Review:* "Growing Distance"

*The Dirty Napkin:* "Self Exam"

*Tipton Poetry Journal:* "Constellation"

*Tule Review:* "Lost in Flight", "Incantation"

*Untitled Country Review:* "Long Haul"

*Up the Staircase Quarterly:* "To Iraq"

*Wild Goose Poetry Review:* "I Need to Make Something"

# GLASS LYRE PRESS, LLC

*"Exceptional works to replenish the spirit"*

**Poetry collections
Poetry chapbooks
Select short & flash fiction
Occasional anthologies**

Glass Lyre Press is a small independent literary press interested in work which is technically accomplished and distinctive in style, as well as fresh in its approach and treatment. Glass Lyre seeks writers of diverse backgrounds who display mastery over the many areas of contemporary literature, writers with a powerful and dynamic aesthetic, and ability to stir the imagination and engage the emotions and intellect of a wide audience of readers.

The Glass Lyre vision is to connect the world through language and art. We hope to expand the scope of poetry and short fiction for the general reader through exceptionally well-written books which call forth our deepest emotions and thoughts, delight our senses, challenge our minds, and provide clarity, resonance and insight.

www.GlassLyrePress.com

CPSIA information can be obtained
at www.ICGtesting.com
Printed in the USA
FSHW012332130219
55663FS